# Dear Parent:
## Your child's love of reading starts here!

Every child learns to read in a different way and at his or her own speed. You can help your young reader improve and become more confident by encouraging his or her own interests and abilities. You can also guide your child's spiritual development by reading stories with biblical values and Bible stories, like I Can Read! books published by Zonderkidz. From books your child reads with you to the first books he or she reads alone, there are I Can Read! books for every stage of reading:

**SHARED READING**
Basic language, word repetition, and whimsical illustrations, ideal for sharing with your emergent reader.

**BEGINNING READING**
Short sentences, familiar words, and simple concepts for children eager to read on their own.

**READING WITH HELP**
Engaging stories, longer sentences, and language play for developing readers.

**READING ALONE**
Complex plots, challenging vocabulary, and high-interest topics for the independent reader.

**ADVANCED READING**
Short paragraphs, chapters, and exciting themes for the perfect bridge to chapter books.

**I Can Read!** books have introduced children to the joy of reading since 1957. Featuring award-winning authors and illustrators and a fabulous cast of beloved characters, I Can Read! books set the standard for beginning readers.

A lifetime of discovery begins with the magical words **"I Can Read!"**

*Visit www.icanread.com for information on enriching your child's reading experience.*
*Visit www.zonderkidz.com for more Zonderkidz I Can Read! titles.*

# HOORAY!

_____

can read this book!

ZONDERkidz

# I Can Read!

SHARED MY First READING

The Beginner's Bible

# Bible Story Favorites

# "I'll teach all of you about God's power. I won't hide the things the Mighty One does."

## –Job 27:11

ZONDERKIDZ

*The Beginner's Bible: Bible Story Favorites Collection*
Copyright © 2011 by Zondervan. All Beginner's Bible copyrights and trademarks
(including art, text, characters, etc.) are owned and licensed by Zondervan of
Grand Rapids, Michigan.

Requests for information should be addressed to:
*Zonderkidz, Grand Rapids, Michigan 49530*

ISBN  978-0-310-72829-0

*The Beginner's Bible Adam and Eve in the Garden* ISBN 9780310715528 (2008)
*The Beginner's Bible Baby Moses and the Princess* ISBN 9780310717676 (2009)
*The Beginner's Bible Joseph and His Brothers* ISBN 9780310717317 (2009)
*The Beginner's Bible Jonah and the Big Fish* ISBN 9780310714590 (2007)
*The Beginner's Bible Jesus Saves the World* ISBN 9780310715535 (2008)

*Illustrator: Kelly Pulley*
*Editor: Mary Hassinger*
*Cover and interior design: Diane Mielke*

*Printed in China*

12  13  14  15  16 /DSC/  10  9  8  7  6  5  4  3  2

zonderkidz. **I Can Read!** SHARED / My First / READING

The Beginner's Bible

# Adam and Eve in the Garden

pictures by Kelly Pulley

God saw all that he had made, and it was very good.
And there was evening, and there was
morning—the sixth day.
—*Genesis 1:31*

In the beginning,
the world was empty.
But God had a plan.

"I will make
many good things,"
God said.

On day one God said,
"I will make day and night."
So he did.

On day two God split
the water from the air.
He said, "Here are the sky
and the sea."

God made land on day three.

Plants grew on the land.

Fruit trees grew there too.

On day four God put the sun
and the moon in the sky.

On day five
God made birds
to fly in the sky.

He made fish to swim
in the ocean.

Day six was busy too.
God made the rest
of the animals.

Then God made the first man.

God named him Adam.

God loved Adam.

God rested on day seven.

He was so happy!

Adam was happy too.

God put Adam in a garden.

The garden was called Eden.

Adam took care of Eden.

He took care of the animals.

He even named all the animals.
"You will be called a 'parrot.'
You will be called a 'butterfly.'"

One day God made Eve.

She helped Adam take care of

the garden and the animals.

God gave Adam and Eve one rule.
God said, "Do not eat
fruit from this tree."

Later, a sneaky snake
was in the tree.

"Eve, you can eat this fruit.
It is fine!" the snake said.

Eve ate the fruit.

Then Adam ate the fruit too.

God was sad.

They had broken his one rule.

This was called a "sin."

"Eve gave me the fruit,"
Adam said.

"Snake tricked me," Eve said.

God said, "Snake,
you must move on your
belly and eat dust."

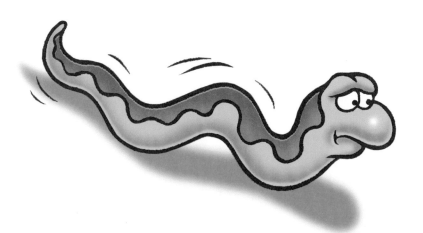

God told Adam and Eve,
"You must leave.
You did not follow my rule."

Adam and Eve left the garden.
They were very sad.

But God would always love them.
He made another plan.

One day, God would send Jesus.
Jesus would save everyone
from their sins.

# Baby Moses and the Princess

pictures by Kelly Pulley and Paul Trice

She opened it and saw the baby.
He was crying. She felt sorry for him.
"This is one of the Hebrew babies," she said.

—*Exodus 2:6*

Miriam lived with her family.

They lived in a land
with a mean king.

Miriam had a baby brother named Moses.

Miriam loved her brother.

One day, Miriam saw
her mom crying.

"Why are you crying?"
Miriam asked.

"The king said he would
take away our baby boy,"
said her mother.

"We must hide Moses
to keep him safe,"
said her mom.

It was hard to keep

Moses a secret.

Sometimes he cried.

Miriam was afraid.

The king might hear Moses.

"God will take care of Moses,"
said Miriam's mother.

Miriam's mom made a basket
for baby Moses.

Miriam's mom put the basket
in the river.

She put Moses in the basket.

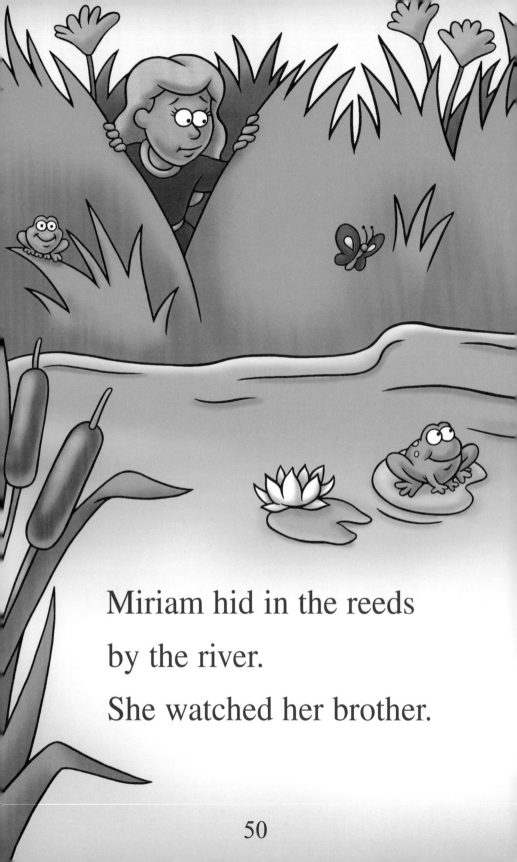

Miriam hid in the reeds
by the river.
She watched her brother.

"Please take care
of my brother,"
Miriam prayed to God.

The river rocked the basket.

Moses did not cry.

God watched over Moses.

Soon the king's daughter
came to the river.

The princess and her helpers
walked next to the river.
She pointed at the basket.

"What is in that basket?"
asked the princess.

"I will get the basket for you,"
said a helper.

Then Moses started crying.

The princess felt sorry
for the baby.
She rocked Moses.

Miriam watched the princess
and prayed.
"God, please keep Moses safe."

The princess said,
"What a cute baby boy!
I want to keep you."

Miriam ran to the princess.
"My mom can take care
of this baby for you."

The princess asked Miriam's mom
to take care of baby Moses.
Miriam and her mom were happy.

When Moses was older,
he went to the king's palace
to live with the princess.

That was God's plan.

God had more plans for Moses.
One day, Moses would save
God's people from the king.

# I Can Read!
### My First
SHARED READING

The Beginner's Bible®

# Joseph and His Brothers

pictures by Kelly Pulley

When his brothers saw that their father
loved him more than any of them,
they hated him and could not
speak a kind word to him.

—*Genesis 37:4*

Jacob had many sons.

He loved Joseph the best.

Jacob gave Joseph a robe.

Joseph's brothers were mad.

They wanted a robe too.

One day, Joseph took food
to his brothers in the fields.

"Last night, I had a dream,"
said Joseph.
"You all bowed down to me."

Some of his brothers
didn't like Joseph's dream.
They wanted to hurt Joseph.

One brother said,

"Do not hurt him.

Let's send him away."

They sold Joseph to some men.

The men took Joseph far away.

Joseph was put in jail.

But God took care of Joseph.

Joseph met a man in jail.

The man said,

"I used to work for the king."

The man said,

"Last night, I had a dream.

I gave a drink to the king."

"What does my dream mean?"
the man asked.

"God knows about your dream.
It means you will work
for the king again," said Joseph.

Joseph was right.

A few days later,

the man got out of jail.

The man went to work
for the king again.

Soon the king had a dream.
"What does it mean?" he said.

"Joseph can tell you what
your dream means,"
said the man.

The king let Joseph
out of jail.

Joseph said, "Lots of food
will grow for seven years.
Then food will stop growing.

God wants us to save food now
so we won't be hungry later."
So the people saved up food.

Joseph was right.

After seven years, the food

stopped growing.

Joseph's family had no food.

They went to the king for help.

The brothers bowed to Joseph.

They did not know it was him.

"I am your brother!"
Joseph said.

"Do not be scared.

I forgive you," said Joseph.

"This was part of God's plan.

God sent me here to help.
God's people did not go hungry,"
said Joseph.

"God is good!"
Joseph and his brothers
cheered.

# Jonah and the Big Fish

pictures by Kelly Pulley

And the Lord commanded the fish,
and it vomited Jonah onto dry land.

—*Jonah 2:10*

# Jonah told people about God.

One day, God told Jonah
to go on a trip.

God said, "People in Nineveh are doing bad things. Please go there and talk to them."

Jonah was not happy.

He did not want to go.
So he ran away!

Jonah talked to some men.
"Please let me sail away
with you."

The boat went out to sea.

It went right into a storm!

The wind blew and blew.

The waves went up and down, up and down.

The men were scared.

"Where is Jonah?" they called.

Jonah was taking a nap.

"Get up, Jonah," they said.
"We are in big trouble!
Say a prayer for us!"

"I am the problem," said Jonah.

"God is upset. I ran away
from him!" Jonah said.

"He wants me to go back. He wants me to go to Nineveh."

"How do we stop this storm?"
asked the men.

Jonah said,
"You must throw me
into the water."

The men tossed Jonah
into the water.

The storm stopped.

The sea was calm!

But up from the water
swam a big fish.

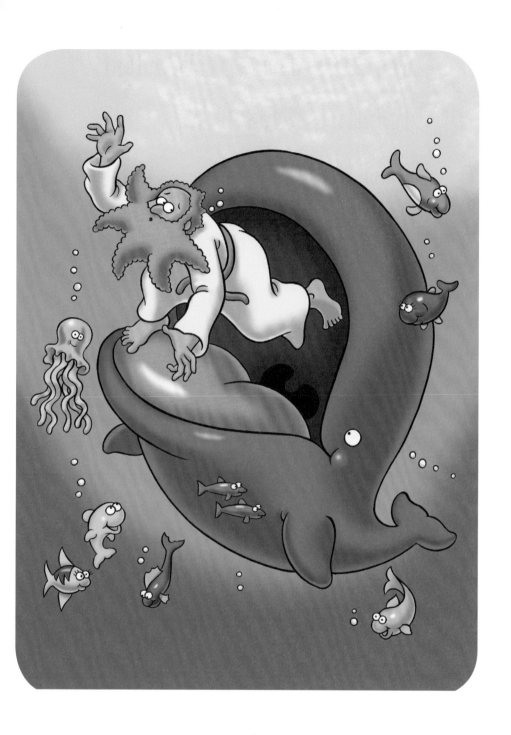

The fish swallowed Jonah.

Jonah sat in the big fish
for three days
and three nights.

"I am sorry I ran away.
Thank you for saving me,"
said Jonah.

Then God said, "Big fish!
Put Jonah back on dry land!"

God said, "Jonah, go to
Nineveh. Tell the people
to stop doing bad things."

This time Jonah was brave.

He knew God was with him.

Jonah went to talk

to the people of Nineveh.

Jonah told the people,
"Stop doing bad things!"

# They listened to Jonah.

God forgave Jonah.

God forgave the people.

He loves all his people.

I Can Read! My First SHARED READING

The Beginner's Bible

# Jesus Saves the World

pictures by Kelly Pulley

"Jesus answered, 'I am the way and the truth and the life.
No one comes to the Father except through me.'"
—*John 14:6*

The day Jesus was born
was a very special day.

Angels came to tell the
good news!

People were so happy
Jesus was born.

Jesus was born to save us from our sins.

Jesus grew up.

He was a good boy.

He helped his mother, Mary.

He helped his father, Joseph.

Jesus helped other people too.

When he was grown,
his cousin John
baptized him.

Then Jesus went to work.

He told people all about God.

Jesus told his friends
about God too.

Jesus' friends helped tell
others about God's love.

Jesus told the people
to love each other.

Jesus also did things
called "miracles."

One day, Jesus and his friends were in a boat.
It started to storm.

His friends were scared.

"Jesus, can you help?" they cried.

Jesus said, "Stop, Storm."

The storm stopped.

It was a miracle!

Jesus also healed people.
He helped a sick little girl
get better. Another miracle!

Jesus healed blind people.

"I can see!" the man said.

Jesus loved all children.

Even when he was very busy,

he stopped to talk to them.

But not all people loved Jesus.
Some made a plan to stop him.

Jesus went to a garden.

He prayed,

"I will do what you want, God.

I am ready to give my life
to save people
from their sins," he said.

The bad men took Jesus away.

They nailed Jesus to a
big cross made of wood.
He died on the cross.

Everyone who loved Jesus
was very sad.

They put his body in a tomb.

Soldiers watched over it.

Jesus' friends went to the tomb.

An angel said to them,
"Jesus is not here.
He is risen!"

Soon, Jesus went to
see his friends.
They were so happy!

Then it was time for Jesus
to go to heaven.
But he will come back one day!

**The Beginner's Bible**
**Timeless Children's Stories**
Illustrator: Kelly Pulley

Introduce children to the stories and characters of the Bible with this beloved and bestselling Bible storybook! With vibrant art and compelling text, more than ninety Bible stories come to life. Kids ages six and under will enjoy the fun illustrations of Noah helping the elephant onto the ark, Jonah praying inside the fish, and more, as they discover *The Beginner's Bible*® just like millions of children before. *The Beginner's Bible*® is the winner of the Retailers Choice Award in Children's Nonfiction.

For online games, fun activities, and teaching resources, visit www.TheBeginnersBible.com. And to hear what others are saying and receive exclusive offers, become a fan of The Beginner's Bible Facebook page!

Available in stores and online!

**The Beginner's Bible Deluxe Edition**
**Timeless Children's Stories**
Illustrator: Kelly Pulley

The bestselling Bible storybook of our time—with over six million sold—is now available in a deluxe edition that includes two audio CDs enhanced with compelling narration, music, and sound effects that help bring more than ninety Bible stories to life like never before.

For online games, fun activities, and teaching resources, visit www.TheBeginnersBible.com. And to hear what others are saying and receive exclusive offers, become a fan of The Beginner's Bible Facebook page!

Available in stores and online!

**The Beginner's Bible for Toddlers: Board Book Edition**
Illustrator: Kelly Pulley

The Beginner's Bible® is the perfect starting point for
toddlers to learn about God's Word. With simple text,
bright art, and a padded cover, this cute board book edition
presents ten Bible stories in bite-sized chunks that kids can
understand. Help toddlers discover The Beginner's Bible®
just like millions of children before!
For online games, fun activities, and teaching resources,
visit www.TheBeginnersBible.com. And to hear what others
are saying and receive exclusive offers, become a fan of
The Beginner's Bible Facebook page!

Available in stores and online!

## Series: I Can Read! / The Beginner's Bible

Beloved stories from *The Beginner's Bible*® are available in the I Can Read, My First level stories for young readers. Accompanied by vibrant art and compelling text from The Beginner's Bible®, these stories from the Bible are full of life and fun, and children can start reading about the adventures of their favorite Bible characters all by themselves!

Complete List of Titles:
*Adam and Eve in the Garden**
*Noah and the Ark**
*Jonah and the Big Fish**
*Baby Moses and the Princess*
*Jesus Feeds the People*
*Baby Jesus Is Born*
*The Lost Son*
*Moses and the King*
*Queen Esther Helps God's People**
*Jesus and His Friends**
*David and the Giant**
*Daniel and the Lions**
*Jesus Saves the World**
*Joseph and His Brothers*
*These titles are also available in Spanish/English bilingual versions!

For online games, fun activities, and teaching resources, visit www.TheBeginnersBible.com. And to hear what others are saying and receive exclusive offers, become a fan of The Beginner's Bible Facebook page!

Available in stores and online!